A POETRY QUINTET

A POETRY QUINTET

POEMS

by

Angus Nicolson, Valerie Owen,
James Sutherland-Smith,
Georgina Hammick, and I. P. Taylor

LONDON . VICTOR GOLLANCZ LTD . 1976

© Angus Nicolson 1976
© Valerie Owen 1976
© James Sutherland-Smith 1976
© Georgina Hammick 1976
© I. P. Taylor 1976

ISBN 0 575 02156 X

PRINTED IN GREAT BRITAIN
BY EBENEZER BAYLIS AND SON LIMITED
THE TRINITY PRESS, WORCESTER, AND LONDON

ACKNOWLEDGEMENTS

Angus Nicolson:
Akros; BBC Radio; BBC TV Scotland; Cracked Lookingglass; Eboracum; Lines Review; Pembroke Magazine (North Carolina); The Honest Ulsterman; The Scottish Review.

James Sutherland-Smith:
Confrontation; Gallery; Omens; Stand; Tangent. I would also like to thank and dedicate this selection to Poet's Workshop and Poetry Round for providing perceptive and encouraging criticism of my poetry.

Georgina Hammick:
Outposts; P.E.N. Anthology 1975; Poetry 2 (Arts Council).

I. P. Taylor
Delta; Encounter; Green's Magazine (USA); Little Word Machine; London Magazine; Outposts; Poetry 2 (Arts Council); Stand; Tribune; Workshop New Poetry; The Stroud Festival International Poetry Competition 1975.

CONTENTS

Angus Nicolson

alasdair's soliloquy
autumn
thoughts concerning the fish salesman, expressed by his workers, in whispers
jean the tinker's letter, drafted by the minister from her dictation, to her daughter married in canada
mart
the gravediggers
country life
calum beag's flock
locked doors
the young have left
cnoc uaine

Valerie Owen

Negatives
Snow Love
The Stones of Venice
The Waves of Light
We Admire and Lament
'Admirers, Importers, Obedient Persons . . .'
The Letter
Blue Ghosts

JAMES SUTHERLAND-SMITH

Preparation for a Mural
The Executioner
Grünewald's 'Pair of Lovers'
Smithfield
Chesil Beach
Things in Themselves
Ravens
Rooks and Michaelmas Daisies
Noise
The Bakery
To an Eleven Year Old Boy Unable to Speak More than
Two Words

GEORGINA HAMMICK

Season of Mists
Bricks
The Prisoner
A Cure for Toothache
A Shortage of Doctors
Queen
Lily
Terminal Disease, Long Sutton
No Pretence Needed
Encounter at Unsted Park Nursing Home

I. P. TAYLOR

Wakers
Crouched
High Hamer

The Scorned
Stormed
When Beasts Most Graze
90°F
Trapper's Dream
Bat Poem
Shoot

ANGUS NICOLSON

alasdair's soliloquy

    1

this
is where i earn my bread.

across this desk, through glass
i see trawlers
dock
    unload
        and sail
while i sell
tickets to sea-travellers with cars
(tourists, gaelic   drunks and ministers),
i see men in yellow coats and black waders
mending nets.
gulls hover   wheel
and perch on mast-tops.
twice daily i hear the ferry's sharp
impatient hoot
at fishing-boats that crowd her berth,
the clock drifts slowly slowly to that moment
when my pen will make its last full stop
in this eight hour century.

    2

in my skiff silkie
there are no clocks or pens,

i drift, net
           herring, pot
                     lobsters, follow
the solan   who know
where mackerel shoal,   and
on dark nights after rain, i may steal
into the lax
           estuary where i will take
many fat salmon.

i am a man upon the sea. i know
every bank between
                     waternish and hunish
and every sgeir. i am
not afraid of storm
or calm. my boat
is sturdy, and i am patient.

3

i am a man upon the land
and this
is where i earn my bread.

across this desk, through glass
i see the silkie
taut against her anchor-chain.

autumn

        she, being the youngest
        girl in the village, said
        thirty winters is too long
        to wait, next summer no-
        one might come, and hitched up
        her skirt to a drunken fisherman
        behind the peatstack.

        i'll blame it on your beautiful eyes
        she said, and the way you dance.

thoughts concerning the fish salesman, expressed by his workers, in whispers

        he's a fullbellied cod
        among cuddies, said wee donald, i'm
        glad i'm not him. the sharks
        will get him, or the tax-
        man's net.

        we can't hook
        him though, said sandy, we're
        the cuddies.

        if the tide
        were strong enough, said red
        murdo, we could beach him. we
        can make that tide.

        eels are the serpent
        of the sea, said peter
        the deacon, and you
        are a dangerous man.

        i have a bit of a thirst,
        said calum the poacher, it's opening time.

jean the tinker's letter, drafted by the minister from her dictation, to her daughter married in canada

    we have been given
                    this cage of roots
    on a hard hinge between
    sea and mountain, a house that does not fold
    like canvas, an acre of stony ground.

    the horse is dead.

    springtides lick
    the blue and gold off
    our old dray that is leaning on broken wheels.

    we don't make now,
    we don't travel,
    there's no market for milkpails
    among such tall weeds.

    eoghan is in finlay's, trading
    his dole for a few
    dreams.

    he'll come home on a cart
    with broken wheels, pulled by
    a dead horse
               then he'll beat me, as if i
    were to blame for the empty byres and his
                                stooped back.

    this house puts knives in our bones.

mart

       some of these farmers loved
       their livestock more than men.
       some were spare crofters, who would taste
       wealth for a few hours. norman,
       fullbacked as his herd, knew he'd sing
       golden songs to the moon but
       lament at dawn. stooped willie spilled
       libations of words over his black family.

       once a year their m.p. came
       to speak. from the dungy platform
       of a cart, his lowland tongue shaped
       prophecies like silver
       mists. only willie
       questioned him. willie could see
       the black side of the moon, weeds
       untameable on each patch
       he sowed.

       the m.p. came to hear the villagers'
       complaints. few complained
       having made fat
       pockets out of fat stirks.
       except old willie, prodding
       his unsold beasts
       homeward. willie's years
       were always lean
       as the fields
       his cattle nibbed.

at night, in finlay's bar, highpriced
hundredweights were cheered
in wanton transubstantiation.
but, in his darkened room,
despising such pale vanities
old willie bruised his knees
to a hard
         unfruitful god.

the gravediggers

>
> willie knew the world would end. he
> prophesied it, today four men cut
> out a green rectangle. four spades
> shape his bed.
> old angus, kenny, jack and alec dig
> until their spades hit rock, then
> pick the rotting rock to gravel, for willie
> must lie deeper. four hours
> they dig, till the turf is shoulder high. they talk
> of anything but death.
>
> tomorrow they, his
> brother and his nephews,
> will hold the cords that lower
> him, and will drop tears
> according to the old ritual.
> today they scatter jokes among the earth
> as if it is a foundation-trench
> they are digging.

country life

      GOD DAMN this earth. when not alive
      with stones it's bog, and always greedy
      for dung. there aren't cows here
      to shit a breakfast for spiky acres
      that clamour for feast.

      not since the great war
      have i had peace. each year
      this place commits me
      to trench warfare.
      and what i win, i lose.

      it broke my beth, long time ago, it drove
      our sons away. she's dead
      who with me made that dyke
      with stones we broke
      from the tillage.
                      and still the wind
      lays flat the half-ripe corn,
                        and still
      it's stony ground,
      and still, each year i scrape
      a few potatoes from among the stones.

      and now that man
      in the big black shining limousine, he says the land
      is his, whom i've never seen
      before. he wants to rob
      me of over fifty years
      of sweat and pain.

this is the only war i know, how can i
make him understand
i am too old for armistice.

calum beag's flock

        that dozen sheep
        was once a gross
        but twenty years have passed
        since a dry fever crept
        into his bones.

        they are good / sheep, fat-
        flanked, heavy with wool
        —but fenced in by
        his infirmity.

        once they had
        the moor, and he
        from conon could name each
        ewe on skudaborg.
        he calls them daily to
        a sack of oats.

        eleven pairs, one prile
        of lambs this year, though his
        crook is now a crutch
                      and the park gate latched
        till market day.

locked doors

1

she always wears three coats, each
moulting, matted into other, keeps
a flock of scrawny
hens, eleven cats, and all
her cash in earthen jars.

murdo died
two years ago. last year she lost
the front door key.
meets neighbours at the back door now,

sees enemies in the garden
thieves among tall weeds.

2

she nurses pus-eyed kittens
till they die, tends dying chickens
(nursed murdo's crippled sister
twenty years), forbids
a neighbour's scythe
to touch the weeds.

morag knows who stole the money
she's mislaid,
buys henfood, meat

to feed the cats, and
rarely eats.

at dusk, she calls
her livestock from the hill, then
locks the door.

the young have left

the young have left
a place propped up on the frail
bones of pensioners.
crofts die under docken thistles nettles and
the absence of livestock.

jack, the youngest tenant, crouching into middle age, reads
history and the "farming news" and keeps
his seven acres green.

elsewhere 'bed and breakfast' signs
invite the traveller to share
a traditional croft cuisine
bought from liptons mobile shop.
small gardens, bordered lawned and free from
hoofmarks, are hedged to hide
the wilderness beyond.

toward the sgeir, the house where andrew lived
is empty
mary peggy's roof has fallen in.

cnoc uaine

grass is coarse here. thistles
flourish. dandelions abound, and foxgloves
like an army on parade are taller
than the drystane outer wall

at the top of one low
oblong mound a lily's
drooping head, its yellow petals
brown-edged, mucuous

beside a fallen marble slab
a sheep's skull
a sparrow-hawk's
and the rusty head of a spade

and there are walls within
where matter rots unseen

there's not much to be said
this
on the crest of a brae
is the place of the dead

VALERIE OWEN

Negatives

To enter an old postcard album.
To be a calm, low-breasted, pale-faced woman,
hour-glassed in a muslin Hardy gown. Her chariot-child
in a starched, pearl-buttoned coat.
    To stand by a small horse-drawn roller.
    To ignorantly lapse on banks, rank with
    wildflower scents. To spit in the dust, on a
    warm woodbine afternoon, gravid
with unravished tombstones. To smell
horse-droppings rolling down the spired sides
of the new London Bridge. To believe
that novelty is progress, increase good,
    that paintings should be like
    and verse should rhyme, that discreet nudes
    are sanctified by Art. That the Apocalypse
    is a sweet dream for pious women.
Today the smart and distant cars
are whining like old rein-held trams.
I have a longing to be anywhere, at any time,
on such a day but where I am.
    But I admit this latest trio of the years
    is also sanctified and put away,
    with recent fears and terrors filed in archives,
    it will become an artefact.
Rôle-playing, with dull-metalled tweezers,
I pick up orange strips and smile.
Never, I think, on static negatives
were heard the obscene murmurings of heart-outrage.

Snow Love

    At eight, a blackbird wore
      white flake-fur on his tail.
    At nine, the snow stood high on twigs,
      a two-inch high grey pall
    which smelled of attic-vapours,
      impossible amours.
        At ten, the echoes misbehaved
          and passed right through the walls.
        Drunken in my book-fields,
          Magritte plough-trains rolled.
        At noon, one alarm-bird chuttered
          and the housewife sun came out
        to prod the once-white house
          now yellow as a bun.

At three, again the vertigo
  which I had felt before at seven
seeing those flakes of falling blood
  purple against the whitened element.
Giddily I slid down with them
  a proxy who enjoyed with you
the passion of the rocking-horse
    outside in the clown-white garden,
      ignominiously frisked
        by mad gangs of breath-bright atoms
      in me knifing peppermint wounds
        of well-fielded unsought passion,
      feathering your far-off flesh,
        bringing me each bolt-sung death.

The Stones of Venice

>
> Into this kingdom I still come.
> My passport is a trick of my mind's pulse.
> The longitudinal screen rolls out for me
> crumbling cohesions, Turner suns, water,
> dog-shit, bodies of the golden gods
> who (their amorous acts performed to Mozart)
> > roll in music, roll in love.
> > A listening travelling bag
> > turns up its gaping mouth
> > towards the coffered ceiling.
> > I run my moistened finger
> > on the sharp edge of your heart
> where rapid cog-wheels spin.
> The pigeons are a bridge between two worlds
> and I have bought them out with me,
> into the air they crack like fans
> above young girls dressed up from head to feet
> in textile flowers.
> > Long golden dresses swing and blow
> > outside arcades.
> > The cold is present. Its touch extends
> > and crisps the harvest blades of pet-dog fur,
> > the lustred leaves in which the copper beech
> > holds tiny flowers.
> Red-velvet target shields hold shining rings
> in stage-door dusk. I follow on
> beyond the concrete fields
> to where with string-tied prams
> the homeless small Napoleons trudge.
> Film pigeons, purloined absent-mindedly,

span these brick-vaulted waters
and the dark canals within my heart.
They roof two towns,
one where we watched the summer come
with crisp dry beetles from the wood
and heard, beneath floor boards,
arpeggios of rats. There
the smell of one's own urine seemed a friend.
I remember still
the well of the sheer wall-cliffs,
myself pale on a window-sill,
the babe tilted forward to catch a slant of light.

The Waves of Light

      Walking noon pavements
      where fine sand describes
      the optical space
      dizzied by roses
      among train-guard crows
      and nibbling sparrows
      who chew every minute,
          walking to girlhood
          beneath powdered hair
          go passing clown ladies
          in bright-eyed blazers,
          swinging
          polythene bags
          of bowling gear
      in afternoons
      where heat
      perpetually shimmers
      and I smell
      the scorching
      of love
      and fame burning
          where the glitter-flies
          moat the dust-gulliver air,
          where
          ten beat-fine thousand sheets
          adhere to fool's breath
          in the underlight's gold-yellow.
      Where Tom
      nyloned with bride-wings
      leans from a window

in noon's paper smile
as Ted points his ladder
up to
the sky.
 Listening to him
 I careless wash
 your summer shirts
 not noticing
 their still-furled cuffs
 and outdoors must
 their attitudes unravel
hearing how
Tom hankers
to be back
in London
painting houses in Park Lane
in his trade
a mark of great distinction.
 Small pink clouds
 dry over smoke-trails,
 shot-satin purple rocks
 mince on their high-spurred
 cow-boy boots
 with a craftman's precision.
Purple is
the colour
of summer,
the star-breath clover,
the shine
round the rooks'
grizzled beaks
 somehow bringing
 the world in to me,
 all the cathedrals

of tourist Europe
in the transistor air
full of the rich souls of workmen
and egg-weskitted bees.

We Admire and Lament

This then our marriage
while you on one knee
with your camera posed
shoot like a toy-soldier
the beaded Sioux mittens
> as I with Tecumseh lament for the vanished,
> cry, where are the people?
> Outside in the street the spraymen arrive,
> guiding the navy and orange ant-eaters.
> They poison the grass-blades
round the stones in the pavement.
Where are the Pequot?
Where is the Mohican?
How is good Joan?
Where is the cottage where Mrs Swift sat,
> smoothing her tight-skinned, arthritic thighs?
> Black stars of confetti fall on my hand
> from the old papered walls.
> There is an aroma of gum and spices,
> there is a quivering burned-varnish haze
and I ask,
where do they store the roof-tiles of love
and the levelled hills, now gone, now gone
as Literature's year-snow melts in the sun?
In the ruin is weeping.
> Where is the gold-friend?
> Where are the things which were scattered?
> Where are the mourned stucco structures?
> 'Acquired by our clients, for redevelopment'
> the dying bells keen in outmoded towns, as

wearing my Indian scarf of sorrow
arriving too late at shops gagged and boarded,
the wind sways the stance of the dusk-time birds
as Tecumseh cries,
'Will we be destroyed?'
  From a window grey as an old cat's ear
  he asks, when fifteen blue screens vibrate
  (the small rolling tears
  fringing his multiplied, sad, leather face),
  'where are the Pequot, where is the Mohican?'

'Admirers, Importers, Obedient Persons . . .'

I always think of you when passing Eros
seeing the way the water floats and leaks
over the paving-steps where now your young men sit
and stare
into a poster-dream of nature,
    thinking
      'one cup is not enough,
      such rugged taste and elegance
      should operate within my blood,
      each corpuscle cracker-stamped
      with real and nourishing letters.'
Behind the dream,
behind the quaintness
of the Index of Design,
cold farmers hack out
child-size graves in each repeated
February thaw.
    I always think
    we search for mortal pieces
    of your soul
    within the white walls of this
    fashionable store
    hiding detectives operating
behind the salt-glaze crocks
and coverlets of natural linen.
Where tired old men buy for
grandchildren's weddings
copies of stoneware pudding-basins,
archaic mincers, flowered jugs
    their grandmothers threw out

     when newer artefacts came in.
     Oh, holiday Walt Whitman,
     was ever life so pretty? Colour-film
     and supplement boy, a country store
     in summer.
Still do I travel, Walt, with thee,
imagine that I wear
your genuine eighteen-fifty denim
of sea-green, ink-blue prussian
bought from a store of hardware,
candies, books and crocks.
     Outside, seeing a bee struggle into life
     upon the city concrete,
     you come to me in cherry trees
     spotting their white-swiss way down
     into valleys
     past country boys with milkdrops on their chins,
pondering the morality of joy,
making innumerable statements
ledgered from the multiplicity of life,
which, far from the chalk-spot dust
of spring,
we catalogue within our merchandise
     buying an expensive dream of travelling salesman,
     balsams, berries, flower-extracts,
     as we face the stare of couches
     through glass windows
     while the speechless purple lovelight
     finally trembles into dusk.

The Letter

Wish
you were here as I now walk delirious this old street
under clearings of blue-jean sky as the lorry-clouds
hurry by to the gilt-flaked hills above pavements
dappled white with chewing-gum roses. Julie once walked
here as did Rosetti.
    She too, used to make translations,
    hers for the doctors. Unhappy, she liked to tease them,
    enjoyed, she said, seeing Sunday headlines in their
    pleased, frightened faces. 'Silly lot,' she said,
    'between us we've all these little ones to keep me
    on the straight and narrow.'
Would
say to Monique, 'take them along the cliff, off you go
now. God! A little child shall lead them.' That empty
playground on the hill, always a child falling off the
slide, parabolizing past a vast red sun wildly sinking
in a pale green winter sea.
    How I wished that I could follow. Oh,
    the boredom and the misery. Took in foreign
    students whose mothers, flown out from Europe,
    talked together in the kitchen.
    'How can they cook in a place like this?'
    voicing European words for antediluvian.
Her
rich relatives-by-marriage, saying, 'you're lucky
to have a leaking roof above your heads. I was
reading . . . only this morning . . .' Forgetting even
her first name. 'If you're in town drop in and see me
at the House,' and silently replying, 'no, come to us,

        in heatwaves we can grill you nineteenth-
        century fleas, they breed somewhere in our
        wainscotting.' Our fault, really, thus to be
        dismissed, ideas above our station. Under-
        nourished bodies at the Pestalozzi working.
        Our only bond, genteel poverty.
Her
spouse making pots in the basement. His isolated
commissions from the rich and famous . . . 'the same
regiment as Rex Whistler . . . decent kind of fellow . . .'
Presentation plates made for the doctors. Mistaken
stable tax requiring sweeping out forever.
        Whenever they got up on their feet,
        did herself up in navy-blue
        right up to the crotch, annoying my husband, saying
        crossly, 'next time I'll just refuse to look.' Wrong
        end of the town really for a pottery. Whenever he made
        a contact, oddly enough she was jealous.
Said
'no one dances in England save the very upper and the
very lower classes, different in Europe where the sand
is warm and clean round the Baltic. Everyone
a little drunk at the wine-tastings.' Finally
flew the roost, lives now in Denmark, the children
        growing-up, commuting to England, must feel like
        parcels. Wish you were here, where the creaking rocks
        pull out Emporium drawers full of the flashing and
        burning of riddling fish, the waves conjuring veils
        of phosphorus over white gulls with spread shining
        tails blazing like comets.

Blue Ghosts

Bleak day, snail-grey, the wind
attempting crag-holds on each face
in less than laundered-white
May–Greenwich. To warm myself
I catalogue the sights of jelly-rubber pups
and donkies like foot-wiper mats
    which lie upon the carpet-grass
    surprising and authentic
    among the plastic-matt.
    Below the cranes and tower-blocks,
    the fairground campaniles, lemon striped,
    are narrow Georgian lanes where it seems
as though the town's inhabitants have died.
One slow car slowly scours the streets as though
for signs of life. Frozen and brave
wearing a cotton shirt,
arm-plaster pinned across my breast,
I note a pigeon with a blood-red fracture,
    a toe misplaced and covered with sham caviar.
    I sit beside a wild, rough, yellow flower
    and try to read the dust,
    the crusts of bread, the broken glass,
    the rusted metal hair
    which bleeds into the gutter.
Then I collect blue ghosts
from faded corner shops
whose small advertisements
have turned to shades of azure.
A steel-blue workman sits upon his indigo bench
and smokes a hyacinth pipe.

      Photographed cashmeres
      speak from their discreet cobalt shelves.
      Hairdresser girls invite the passers-by
      with bluebell flesh under a Swansea sky.
      I quote to them, 'Blues don't mean a tempo
      but a structure.'
Yet time does weather structures into art as
the dust splits waves of light into cerulean,
then to the infinite blue of cornflowers past.
The present clouds are long transparent loaves of bread
above this Blücher's bedroom of the homeless.
I've seen them wear the laced-up property boots
      which might have come from early films by Chaplin.
      Down there they lie flat on their cardboard sheets,
      so I cover them with art,
      borrow for them an alien history.
      For white hawthorn I substitute
      the banjo songs of cotton bolls, of weevils
and I sing them my own Greenwich Blues
though the cold, wet prestige lawns now beckon
like fame, that secretary-shielded great unknown.
They call, exciting and uncomfortable as love-acts,
and in the town's low-ceilinged emptiness
their hungerings my hand-held architecture touch.

JAMES SUTHERLAND-SMITH

Preparation for a Mural

for Victor West

You will begin at a wall of pure colour;
Immanent as the yellows you see
When you close your eyes against strong sunlight.
You must remove its pigment carefully
Flake by flake. Underneath there emerges
A portrait of a lover and his mistress.
Their fingers are touching and they stare
At each other with all the mild savagery
Of those whose conversations end 'Perhaps'.
Scrape them off and you will discover
A landscape showing a hunting party.
Stick figures with huge genitals pursue
Hog and antelope. A demon writhes
From a tree-bole threatening quarry and hunter.
Its coils symbolise evil while a straight spear
Pins it to the tree. Above the scene are gods;
Fish, crocodile, lion and ape depicted
In ochre. Whether they were painted
First or added as an afterthought
Is of no consequence. All must be erased
To leave traces of dirt and blood. Wash those off
And place your palm against the pure rock.
You will feel it warming with the earth's heat.

The Executioner

They meet in a museum. Difficulties
Have become inessential, bony, staring
From a glass case. They embrace between displays;
The polished rock crystal of an Aztec skull
And a ceremonial knife's stone haft.

He promises a night of sacrifice
Until, outside by a fountain, she throws
The offering back. 'Words! Words are all
You come to,' letting the clear water
Splash and trickle through her fingers.

He returns to the compelling truth
In his wife and makes for himself a nightmare
Without torso, her head between her legs,
A bearded lady. By morning he is
Formal and serene as text from scripture.

Mineral day! He needs matters to assume
The nature of stone and metal, burnished,
Owing nothing to ore and rust, intentions
And history. He wants that essence achieved
When a guillotine falls through the neck of time.

He contemplates his inconsistencies;
The pines pointing like arrows, the bladed ridge
While his wife's voice strops over him,
Forgiving, so different from that other
Who let the clear water, the clear water.

Grünewald's 'Pair of Lovers'

Shall I say her eyes might have been lovely
And his hands were once smooth and strong
As marble? The rest is pitiful.

Blowflies are their jewels clustering
At sores. Serpents bind them close
One whispering in the man's ear

While another girdles the woman
Gleaming like Aphrodite's belt.
Dragonflies flick over this carrion

And time itself decays. A toad kisses
The woman's sex as her teeth show
In a lipless scream of ecstasy.

The man, modest for a change, holds the sheet
Across his gnawed or shrivelled genitals.
The sheet covers and damns them.

I look at these lovers while you sleep on.
Your breath spirals in the cold air mingling
With mine, the ghost of a snake.

You do not dream of the Great Beast.
Your breathing is too slow for nightmare.
Will I ever say your eyes are lovely?

Smithfield

First you reach a severed calf's head.
One eye trails from it on a string
Of nerves and skin.
                      You walk on the road
Avoiding pavements slimy with blood
And the offals heaped in bulging
Polythene bags.
                 A butcher smiles at you
While he ties up a pig's carcase
Scoring its rind of gristle.
                     You see building
On building, a whole city ribbed with meat.
It is near your blood time.
                     When I ring
You say 'No, no, no! I'm all right!'
Yet you feel yourself distend until you fear
The office walls might crack under the stress
Of your bulk.
             You can only wait sensing
The relief of pain, counting each fat second.

After work you will return through the market
On pavements hosed clean, past porters wearing
Fresh overalls and the rows of empty hooks.
You will walk quickly thin as a blade.

Chesil Beach

for Ruth and Kevin Crossley-Holland

Somewhere near the approaches to feeling
The sea inheres, even converses,
Albeit with shrugs and truisms
Allowing such hints as this glassy
Restlessness to spill on shingle
While behind a bleak pane of water
Hardly seems to fill Weymouth Bay.

Between them the pebble stretch is shifted
As if in response to mood or perhaps
Patterning a reticence before mood.
All the stones on the shore; wry flints,
Enigmatic grits, taciturn basalts
Are smoothed and rounded to perfect shapes
Hiding their first and true nature.

Things in Themselves

The being who can bear to think neither of the past nor the future is reduced to the state of matter.
—Simone Weil

1

Nothing stirs the limes repose.
Their bark stretches dry and coarse
As the skin of white women
Who have lived in the tropics.

Pigeons squat in the mulberry
Surfeited on its blood fruit.

A Virginia creeper
Has unwisely curled from shadow
To murmur love! love!
At the sun's mad eye.

I sit in the garden
Turning over in my hands

A jar you filled with pebbles
And pieces of luminous green glass
Planished by the sea
To a texture of smooth pumice.

2

On the road to Capua I travelled
Fanning myself with hyssop to ward off
The stench of the fruit of Crassus' victory;
Rows of ten times ten times ten.
It's a poor but necessary abstraction
I make to sweeten the memory
Of those slaves twisted on their crosses
A wordless signature of pain, stretching
As far as the eye could bear to see.
Rooks gathered above them and squabbled
Like the rabble on voting day
Or settled and strutted as if to mock
The eagles on our legions' standards.

3

To mortify the flesh is one expedient
Gaining useless perfection. Silence,
Manual work, confessions of small rages
Indicate others. I contemplate my age
But do not count the years since God touched me,
Still unable even to strive to reach him.

4

I've stayed too long in the land of no feeling
Where wounds occur and heal unnoticed.
I am hideous with scar tissue.
Only you remain whole, even more beautiful.

At the swimming pool I watch you dive
And worry about the small danger
From water scorpions. At night my hands scuttle
Across your belly and breasts like cockroaches.

I can recall less and less clearly the time
When to possess, to possess you was a means
Commanding my love, an end I abandon
Since it is enough to watch you laugh
And sit combing water from your hair.

5

In the battle dark other human screams
Placed each shell's blast or else the flashes
Might have been imposed on my retina
By the sheer force of my own thoughts bursting.

As a convalescent, I enjoy
The luxury of distances
Between myself and what I see.
Far off a cadet band slow marches
An intricate drill. I shield my eyes
From the sun's dazzle on serpents and piccolos.
I could listen to their noise forever.

6

The cellar reeks of petrol, spilt stale wine
And the Thames seeping through brickwork.
For a time we give ourselves entirely
To a conveyor belt's ceaseless rustle

And the steady, almost military,
Movement of our arms unloading it.

At lunchbreak a gang clears the warehouse gutters
Of the season's lees; pigeon nests, leaf mould.
I walk through an alley, spattered with eggshells
And fledglings, to watch the ebb tide swill past.

Leaning on a parapet, I notice
My head's outline shadowed above it, a target
For the solitary, maniac marksman
Aiming from high-rise flats across the river.

7

To pull the lever. To pull the lever
Is the thought which obliterates and preserves.
My mother and sisters, looking forward
To the comfort of warm water
From showers, enter the chamber. Impossible
To greet them. I pull the lever and listen
To the hardly audible hissing of gas jets.

Ravens

A raven flew from the Ark
And reported back croaking 'It's no good.
We must have drifted out
Into limitless ocean. Noah,
We must introduce birth control
And live off fish. O, and censor
Irresponsible talk from the dove.'

Later there were ravens to support
Appeasement and Stalin's henchmen
Were reputed to keep them as pets.
Ravens have always liked to stand
On one foot, shifting from the left
To the right in a kind of slow jig
Which they prefer to call wisdom.

Rooks and Michaelmas Daisies

And for you they are performing
A ritual dance to the blue king.
The shadow beneath oaks
Thickens to sheer November blue.
They must give up their own jet-black.
Their wings shiver a colour's tension
Between blue and darkness.
They will fly at you through mist
Screaming the blueness of ploughed turf,
Leaf-mould, the patterns of frost.
Blue. Blue. How it dominates
Even the air's texture, your thought.
Yet these flowers you hold
Their petals enclose blue, subdue blue.

Noise

It is difficult when there is no other
To abide your words or suggest new phrases
With a change of mood. It is no better
To wait by yourself through hours when words
Seem like numerals, not breath and your heartbeat
Is a double-drone not a questioner.

Your neighbour's pigeons prattle with more irony
Than you can muster. The less than human
Begins to speak. A car whispers through rain.
From the hillside an owl's cry elaborates
While its victim screams once. There the drizzle
Is sifted through sheep's fescue and wildcress
Soaking the pasture where you often go
To wait until the music comes for you.

The Bakery

The baker I work with has the name
Of a war poet, is deaf and dumb.
A single labial and gesture
Articulate his purpose while behind
Ovens roar the gas jets' open vowels.

I must mime pain when he passes
A tray too warm to hold. Neither cursing
Nor banter humour his shift as he works
Among women whom years of standing
Have made unattractive and varicose.

They knead and dispense realities
Of love and work without the days
Seeming to be disproportionate
As the swelling dough, becoming
So much air so many racks of baps.

But to tell this to those who praise
Beauty and idleness is as
Unsatisfactory as spreading
A handful of flour and tracing on it
Messages to the deaf and dumb.

To an Eleven Year Old Boy Unable to Speak More than Two Words

Awaking to the smell of varnished oak,
The waterproofed screws fixing the lid tight
So you must scrabble at the wood with your nails
Until earth sags through or your air gives out,
You would shriek 'Door! Door!'

Watching an oak leaf turning an edge
And the flat surface towards you disclosing
And shutting out the spinney's insect whistle,
Watching wasps massed around a hole
Inside a blackberry patch drowsily
Climb the brambles then rise like flak
You would whisper 'Door. Door.'

Seeing eyelids open after sleep
And mouths uttering for you mere noise
Which, for all you know, could be a curse
Or a song you would reply 'Door. Door.'

If you were shown the passages
In the pyramids closing up after
The sand counterweights flow out letting
The dressed blocks settle into place,
The widening decorated arches
Around the engraved wood of an entrance
To a cathedral where sinners take
Their naked worship and if you were shown
The unadorned steel shutters on the grills
In a prison you would observe 'Door. Door.'

You could tell me what is behind me.
It has a frame and panels of pine,
A handle of brass and iron. It is
Painted white although unskilfully
Where the gloss has run and dried in streaks.
'Door,' you would say 'Door. Door.'

GEORGINA HAMMICK

Season of Mists

Our window looks on a November garden
Half put to bed—the dahlias sodden.

Beech, walnut, sycamore and lime
Have lost their leaves, but the elms still hang on

To a sickly few. This perennial
Nightmare of raking! From the flint wall

Untethered Longicuspis trails and whips
Our sad herbaceous, choked by leaves, dog shit
And the vile apples we forgot to pick.

Bricks

He built a high wall round
And shut us out. A lack
Of proper sympathy
Was the reason for it.
Some of the bricks were loose,
But not by accident.

Bored or in need, he would
Remove a brick and shout
Help! through the muffled chink.
And we came, bringing rugs,
Brandy, bandages; all
The essential kit

For arctic survival.
It was not good enough.
We were careless, slow; worse
We dropped things. By the time
We reached him, he'd have the
Brick back, exactly in place.

Pressing an ear to the
Smooth wall, we could not tell
Where the hole had been, could
Hear no sigh or breathing.
He would have us know it
Was not he who had called.

Later, when no one was
Watching, the provisions

Would vanish. Tins thrown in
The grass were evidence
He was alive, but we
Learned not to expect thanks.

And learned, in time, to keep
Our distance, till, almost
Out of earshot, we could
Not be certain we heard
Him. Meanwhile, the rescue
Equipment rusted up.

Perhaps he hoped we'd fetch
A bulldozer and knock
The wall down. He wanted
His bluff called, I think. But
We were too lazy and
Too much afraid of him
For that.

The Prisoner

The princess in the tower
Is waiting for her prince;
She will let down her hair
For him to advance.

He will arrive tonight
And stay in her arms till dawn.
She imagines how his weight
Will drag her head down.

She imagines how his weight
Will pin her to the bed
As the rats run over the floorboards
And the owls hoot overhead.

As the owls hoot in the rafters
And the rats run round the floor,
He will comfort her with kisses
And tell her he loves her more

Than the treasures of his kingdom,
Than his horses and his men—
Who parade every day before breakfast
On the emerald castle lawn.

The princess sits there dreaming
Of how her prince one day
Will rescue her from this prison
And gallop her far away

To the castle in the mountains
Where his horses and his men
Change guard every day at breakfast
And again in the afternoon.

For every time he visits
He brings a skein of silk,
And she's weaving it into a ladder
In the evenings after dark.

The princess stands there ready,
Tightening her rope of hair;
She does not know (as we do)
That the witch will climb the stair.

And because I, in my childhood,
Could hardly bear to look
At the wicked witch and her scissors
In the frightening fairy book

As she snicked the golden tresses
And jeered at the shaven head,
And then waited in a passion
To greet the prince instead—

I'll stop the projector whirring
And freeze the image. Here
Is a girl at the window watching
About to let down her hair.

A Cure for Toothache

>
> Hubbard is slim and handsome in the photograph
> Taken at North West River on the day
> He started out with Wallace whom he loved
> Into uncharted central Labrador. It proved
> A fatal journey for Leonidas
> Hubbard. He never reached his goal, Lake
> Michikamau. Forced to retreat, he died of cold
> And hunger at the point where Goose Creek
> And the Susan River meet. A final
> Photograph, taken outside his camp, shows
> Him a wretched tinker, huddled in the snow
> Among stiff rolls of bedding, useless saucepans.
> His feet, tucked under him, are out of sight.
> The caption tells us they were gangrenous.
>
> Wallace, less handsome in the snap but clearly more
> Robust, survived that first and ill-equipped
> Attempt of Nineteen-Three. He made it finally
> In Nineteen-Five, and later on, in homage to his friend,
> Retraced the original route. At Hubbard's grave,
> His etched memorial on a boulder reads:
> *Leonidas Hubbard, Jnr., Explorer*
> *And Practical Christian, died here* . . .
> The unprofessional lettering shows up well.
>
> Wallace lived on till Nineteen-Thirty-Nine,
> Hero to schoolboys, famous for his books:
> *The Long Labrador Trail*; *The Lure*
> *Of the Labrador Wild*—titles I may have seen
> On nursing-home, Trust House Hotel, or prep-

School library shelves. Something
About them seems familiar—

But Dillon Wallace, Leonidas Hubbard,
Were men I knew nothing of until today.
So was it luck? A hunch?
Made me select *The Beaver, Magazine
Of the North* (published by Hudson's Bay
Co. Inc. of Winnipeg—a quarterly)
As cure for toothache in a waiting-room?
Instead of *Woman's Journal*, say, or *Punch*.

A Shortage of Doctors

Each time, giving birth,
I fell in love
With the midwife.

Three different babies born in
Three indifferent hospitals;
Three different midwives

Who appeared not to be.
What was it that hooked me—
Their briskness? Their uniform

Sense of purpose? 'Push
Harder, there's a good girl'—
I wanted to please them.

Checking a heart beat with
A cold stethoscope, they
Told me jokes. Each time

I thought the pain would kill me.

*

Patients are known
To fall for their nurses,
And all of these

Were young or pretty.
Nevertheless, it
Would seem unusual.

Queen
for Rose

Who is this person
strolling towards us down a green
walk in the garden?
Goodness, it is a Queen.

A Queen in a soft brown
hat and gardening gloves.
She is dead-heading
roses; her features harden

as she approaches with basket
and secateurs. Is she beheading
someone she loves?
To be honest, she looks a bit daft

in that get-up, but Queens
can get away with murder,
sartorially speaking,
and always have done. Even so,

we can tell this Queen is really,
despite that hat and the gumboots
that do not fit her, extremely
Queenly.

She has Queen hair,
Queen eyes, a Queen nose
and a most Queen-
ly expression.

Don't you think so, Rose?

Lily

who died after being attacked
by a greyhound

>She used to sit and watch me write.
>The room was full of fags and smoke.
>I knew her eyes were on my back.
>She knew if she could stare me out—
>When I swung round she didn't blink—
>I'd have to take her for a walk.
>She knew that I adored her white
>Small body with the bits of black
>On ears and tail; her bark; her bite
>That didn't hurt (a sort of joke);
>Her eyes that always stared me out.
>She was attached to me I think.
>
>She was attached to me I know.
>She used to sit and watch me write.
>The room is full of fags and smoke.

Terminal Disease, Long Sutton

To look on the bright side, you could say
(Which is true) there will be more air;
More sun where there used to be shade; views
No-one has seen before.
But I do not like the sound of the saw
And would not choose
This view of a neighbour's pants and concrete
Sheds; the landing-lights on Odiham airfield.

And though, in theory,
Most of us now have wood
To last ten winters,
These logs aren't easy
To get going. (Take five fire-lighters,
Half a ton of kindling . . .)
They hiss, release black smoke, but
Do not actually burn.

Were our elms really dead, that had so much sap in them?
Where will our rooks build now?

Replanting hardwoods will take time; energy; money.
Nobody has any.
And the business of replanting—
Whose is it, exactly?
'The council ought . . .'
'What is the C.P.R.E. there for?'
'We're an elm landscape. We deserve
A government grant . . .'

We have already lost
The elm that served as village notice board;
Five trees by Chaffers' Close—and worse,
The group that proved (May till the end of August)
A natural boundary to the cricket field.
Our elms were huge. Their going throws the church,
The primary school, the rash of yellow, new-
Built bungalows into a harsh relief
That was not meant.
We have already lost an indigenous
Sense of proportion.

Someone must plant soon
Or we shall have left
Only the churchyard yews
Which have stood for a thousand years,
But which suddenly
Look sickly—

And fruit trees in the gardens:
Apple mostly;
A few cherry: pink; double-flowering; not the fruiting sort;
A plum or two;
The odd fig.

Is there a cure
For apathy? Could we inject
Against it?

No Pretence Needed

He knew he was dying, so no pretence
(*Daddy, you know you're looking fine!*)
Was needed when we found him weaker—
Who shrank from sixteen stone
To six in those few months,
And was sick as a dog most days, or sicker—

Yet on his birthday (60th; in May),
One week before the undertakers bore
His coffin out, we stood and watched him try
To unwrap presents: after-shave and soap,
Slippers we knew he couldn't hope to wear—
When all he really needed was to die.

Encounter at Unsted Park Nursing Home

'Excuse me . . . I wonder . . . you look
Well, *young*—the kind of messenger
I have been waiting for. My name,
By the way, is Jack Roper.' Stretching
My legs after a visit here, I walk among
Neat, garish beds of Zambra, Super Star
And Masquerade, and am about to leave.
He comes up imperceptibly, along
A windswept arbour of Dorothy Perkins,
Under a predominantly
Grey sky patched with blue,

And looks the gentleman
He must always have been, erect
And formal in a pale grey suit.
His slow steps require a disciplined effort.
Close to, he smells of lavender
And appears older than God, his
Eyes a washed-out blue, his fleshless
Face wearing a stretched, mottled skin.
A sort of microphone hangs round his neck.

'I wonder . . . it would be most kind . . .
If you could tell the Port Line—
That is, someone on the Board—
It really doesn't matter who—
That I think it's time I was retired,
Put out to grass or on a shelf
Somewhere.' He peers at me and grins.
'I think you'll find they'll be relieved

At my decision. I've done my bit,
Been with them since the 1890s, actually, but
I don't think that *this* year I can cope
With the pressures Autumn always brings . . .

Do you mind my asking this?
There isn't any desperate rush.
It doesn't matter who you talk to.
I'd be most grateful if you could.
I'd like to leave it all to you—
Just who you tell and how . . .
If you could get my message through . . .'
I smile and nod and treacherously agree
To do as he requests; insist
That it's no trouble, that I'd like
To be his messenger. We walk
Together slowly to my car.
He watches me reverse and drive
Away, gives a conspiratorial wave.

He was not mad at all, and did not seem
Senile, though I know he
Must have been. He was a charming man,
Polite, lucid; hesitant because
He did not want to be a bore, to me or
To the 'Port Line', merely felt
He'd done enough and now
Should be allowed to rest somewhere, at grass.
His conversation, in another time—
Say, thirty years ago—
Would have made perfect sense.
But it was odd he did not see the grass
All round him, and did not recognize
This shelf he longed for: dusty; beyond our reach.

I. P. TAYLOR

Wakers

night spills
from the lips of owls

from the squat house knelt
in its grasses moonlight

draws a hand with a cigarette

he waits   the house
can't keep him

he stares through the catweb dark
through the thornlattice

he sees the scrub of frost
on sheds and fencetops

the road goes in silence
or a hare's foot crossing

over miles a vixen screams
her dog carves back

his thoughts track in the frost
to a bed he cannot share

his loneliness bites
on a raw moon

fruit of the night is owls
and the calls of prey

clawstripes in emptiness

Crouched

>with a cry like a shower of plateglass
>he is among us
>
>his voice is a plunge in a cold bath
>
>moonlight along a wall
>might be the gleam of his eye
>
>he drenches the night with a banshee wail
>his will to survive
>
>beyond the dahlias and the box hedge
>twin icefires crackle between kills
>
>somewhere he drags a twitching fur
>squats in a slaver of pheasant eggs
>
>his afternoon spreads on a sunned stone
>lays soft traps in the mouseruns
>fishes the barn floor from a rafter
>
>tomorrow is another assault
>a neat slip from a hotbarrelled keeper
>
>a bleeding knife in air

High Hamer

The house was half sunk in the nettleswamp.

Among cobwebs and the shells of rats
the dark pulse had ached,
left the house to wreck under the wind.
The world had stepped back from the door.
The three were alone.

Peatcutters bunched past,
their eyes fixed to the heather.
They heard the dogs' rage
after rats at the back of the feed
in the barn, mumbled and glanced back
when ten minutes' walk had put up
a fist between them.

Roadsters, like shameless crows,
crossing the brown moor
under the white sky,
saw the girl at the pumphandle
turn a face as pale as first light,
but would not sup in the beck
or stop in the lea of the farm's walls.

An occasional rider—his brain
pelting like a moor hare—passed
in a low mist at evening, bent
at speed, his eye to the track,
hearing the woman's screams
like jets of blood.

In a spring of high wind
and high water the man died—
from a dose enough for all his vermin—
taken away unmourned on a cart, leaving
his clothes to be burned, his tools to be sold.

The wild journeyman surprised asleep
in the barn stayed a week, cut wood,
mended the roof and the chimney,
built up the walls round the field
and took the girl with him—
while the woman slept with the feel
of him still within her.

The tinkers came in the summer—
found the chained dogs' bones in the yard,
the woman aloft in the barn.

The Scorned

      he comes like them for the sea sun

      hunched in his nest of coats
      on a council bench on the cliff

      he is riddled with stares

      picked over by the grins
      and asides of the clean world

      for a self-conscious moment
      anger flickers his fingers

      he might heave a curse
      at them stark and sudden
      as a windbleached bone

      protest a pinebrown fist

      fall from his bench in a fit of rags

      but he endures
      motionless
      his face closed in like a ferret

      his future creeping asleep
      like a full dog in a hot yard

the beach fills with a litter
of bare limbs and torsos

pale people come to the benches
spread sandwiches and flab

he sits
still and black as a dead crow
strung on a keeper's wire

children dare who goes closest

the bikes come in a blast of contumely
slam helmets on the rail behind him

he is oblivious
warm

*

I've seen him on the road
at dusk the fastbacks
leaning the corner near him
clutching his bags to his coat

darker than the hump of night
and rook flight homeward

Stormed

The windows glimpsed it as it sprang—
they stared back stiff as victims.

A wingspread fell across the room like death.

Light shrank to a gash. Wind
beat the eaves like dull artillery.

Beneath the thunderheads, horizon lightning bobbed
like a fevered dream. Trees
staggered there—refugees
from the streaming night clutching their loads.

Dawn was white,
late,
drained.

Inch by inch sounds
squeezed out, to twitch
like severed nerves,
testing air for reassurances—

the taut resetting of normality.

When Beasts Most Graze

1

> *left their houses weeping and became unemployed*
> *and finally . . . died in poverty*
> *and so ended their days*
> —Extract from the Commission of Inquiry
> Returns 1517

Tenant at Will, Wharram Percy. (Circa 1500):

    They found me at Milndam, at the fishpond,
    the landmaster's men. They said:
    Leave your nets, William. We're fishers of men.
    Come with us to the Lord's house. Come—
    and receive the Word.
                    I followed,
    sharp as a fox out of cover. Squire Hilton
    hung like a cloud on his front step.
    His smile axed at my heart.
    He gave me till Michaelmas—
    'Tell the whole village the same.'

    I looked up to the furlongs, the skyline of corn.
    I heard children laugh at the stream.
    I turned from his gate. For Hilton
    a sheep-run. For the cottar
    death with the plough.

Our young men wanted to fight, but
I counselled acceptance: To sever one stoat
will summon the pack. We have no rights here—
leave behind little. Our tears
like our toil will fade into the land.

We gathered below Town Field.
Swallows twitched from the churchtower,
bellied the shallows. Next year
they'll nest in the houses. . . .
Silence will gulp their cries dumb.

2

> *for where there have been a great many householders
> and inhabitants there is now but
> a shepherd and his dog.*
> —Bishop Latimer 1549.

Shepherd of Wharram Percy. (Circa 1501):

Wharram, Octon, Bartindale, Argam
gone—choked under wool. What weighs more
than a sack of wheat?
Why man—a bleat!

I'm lucky, I know. I've moved
to this fine stone house that was William's.
The others are down. The best timber's gone
for the Hall—the rest for the sheep-fence.

Last September groped by like a blind hag.
Most cursed the shepherd—
many the priest. Hilton had need of us both.
Like rabbits we kept to our doors.

I watched them, threading away
down the valley. Bent like a windwhipped thorn,
the priest wept alone in the church.
I crept the Manor lawns, waiting Hilton's command.

3

> *wither shall they go?—*
> *forth from shire to shire*
> *and to be scattered thus abroad.* . . .
> *by compulsion driven some of them*
> *to beg and some to steal.*
>   —Extract from the Sheep Pamphlets.

Former Cottar of Wharram Percy:*

    On the wolds slopes distrust.
    In the towns rejection. At Grimston
    the cottagers stoned us. In Malton
    they barred the doors. To York,
    William said: There'll be work.
    Shelter. A larger place will seclude us.

    But in York there were many like us,
    and a threatening fear among townsmen.

*Skeleton discovered 1951.

Some of us left for the coast. In our camp
by the Derwent old William failed.
On a stretcher of reeds, Thomas and I
bore him back to the village.

In William's cottage the shepherd slept—
thick as a mole in a clod. We hunched
in a doorway. Cold chiselled our bones.
As first-light frosted the hills the slight breathing
                                        stopped.

We laid tumbled turves on the body—
our words too stubborn for prayer.

4

> *But I fancy that the town*
> *has been eaten up with time,*
> *poverty, and pasturage.*
>   —Abraham de la Pryme 1697.

Wharram Percy 1975:

If you ask in the parish they'll tell you the way—
unless they're farmers. Press them,
and they'll say it was taken by plague.
Come in July, to the dig. Learn of the finds
that jog a response to the pulse of the place:
the pair of dice, the bone needle, a thimble,
a coin. . . . Or come in spring,
  when the form of the land is most easily seen:

fasten your boots. For the last half-mile
follow the tractor-ruts. Descend between swallows
cresting the folds of young corn.

The roofless church is alone in the valley—
like an old jaw loose with decay.
To the west, on the scarp-edge,
are the humps of the houses—
shallow graves in the grass.

The wind flows above them—
preserving a sadness restrained over time.

90°F

It hits me like a bombblast.

Eight o'clock:
already the fields blur to water.

The housefront bounces the swell off
like a seacliff. Hoeing beans, I am
a dripping waxwork. My shirt clings like defeat.

A swirling sediment of insects clouds
the stoppered air. Their life-cycles accelerate
toward hysteria. My limbs slow like the drowned.

But I can sense relief—
following the droughtwind's flung coals,
shambling up the greenways like an antique journeyman—

an evening's sudden cool,
a brassy echo from the beechwoods. . . .

autumn gripping the edge of things.

Trapper's Dream

The lake is dazed by the moon.
Black pines rank the soundless edge,
pointing the precipice like minarets.
The amphitheatre ridge—
carved crests of an iron sea—
glints like a signal.

The moon ships oars and coasts.
Her twin, drawn from the lake floor
blandly returns her light.
I spread on my bundled furs,
choked with unspoken metaphor. . . .

But absence is a sullen stone
frozen in me. One month north
I set for wife and home—enough beneath my head
to buy the promises I made.
This boldens my return.

A vast ram of water pushes under me.
My craft, dead on its belly,
like a carcass ravened out,
arrows for the rapid's jaws—
the grill of teeth that crush at the lake mouth,
belch up splinters of uncertain helmsmen.

My nerves snap into one,
sharp with a snaking fear. I hear
the cauldron's hungercall. I crouch,
statued in the prow. The water churns, seethes white,

then down, down—I ski the funnel rim.
Like blood in haematemesis
the flood, swallowed whole, erupts.

The torrent heaves beneath me
like a rising whale. I plunge my oar.
I plunge, I plunge—
But the weight of furs—
The cascade pours
into a knot of wrestling arms.
The boat spins against my grip,
rears for the black tusks like a supplicant—

                The pines,
the mountain ridge, the moon,
leap from my sight—
I am roaring volumes down an endless falls

The birch-ends rekindle
          in a shrill wind cowled with snow.
The carcajou quarrels in the dark.
There is no movement on the lake ice, though
I stare a long time from my tent.

Bat Poem

    I began like a row of beautiful white notes
    played once and sealed perfect

    but my hands sprawled across them
    as I slept
    and the sound broke
    deep wounds in my face

    now I crawl beams
    like a gob of night
    a cold shudder at dusk for gnats

    the ticking beetle rots floors through my sleep
    my night opens in a vomit of moth skulls

    behind the rent of my flight
    the moon claws up her western rope

    I am as cold as moonwash
    the serrated edge of fear

    I have no voice for love

    I am safe so long as I don't change

Shoot

Birds, penned for breeding, fed
all summer from the keeper's hand,
live in this wood.

Today, a line of men sprouts up
between field and trees. Their boots
munch frosted stubble, as the line strings out,
enters the fir-fringe. The men move resolutely.
Their arms carve grotesque gestures, they whoop,
yell, whistle, slap sticks on leggings.
Dogs follow, low at keepers' heels, nostrils
thrilling to the terror-scent ahead.

A dozen guns, sportsman-clad, spaced out
across the beck, tensed for familiar calls
of rusty throats erupting into air—
the multi-coloured wings—prepare
to blast night through the heads of pheasants.

The line of beaters steadily devours the ground
that death will occupy. Dogs
edge forward, poised for runners.

Barred by wire fencing at the wood's end,
thirty feet from the nearest gun,
pheasants thrust for sky.

Small puffs of feathers linger
on the air. Bodies sway among the larchtops,

like rags of last year's nests: beat
upon the ground, into the beck.

The count is made. Guns
attest their hits.

The wood respires. Briars twitch
from trodden earth—restore a skeletal defence.

Biographical Notes by the Contributors

Angus Nicolson
Born 1942 in the Isle of Skye. Left island, school and home at sixteen. In 1968 entered Glasgow University as undergraduate. Edited student magazine G.U.M. Remains undergraduate though no longer at university. Has published regularly in the Scots Gaelic quarterly *Gairm* and in various Scottish, Irish, and American magazines. Has done the usual variety of jobs—gardener, gravedigger, warehouseman, clerk etc. Now working for a community housing association in London. Current member of the General Council of the Poetry Society and National Poetry Centre.

Would like to dedicate this selection to Philip Hobsbaum whose advice 'Go back to your roots' led to the sequence 'rock and water' from which the selection is taken.

Valerie Owen
Valerie Owen was born in Essex where her father was an Arts and Crafts teacher. She studied at the Slade School of Fine Art and the London University Institute of Education and has taught Art in Secondary Schools and Creative Writing and Art History at an Art College.

She has read poems on B.B.C. Radio 3 and contributed to the P.E.N. anthology *New Poems 1973-4*, the Arts Council anthologies *Poetry 1* and *2* and various magazines. New Poets Award Runner-up and Camden Poetry Award joint prize-winner.

She is married, has one daughter and divides her time between Hastings and Croydon.

James Sutherland-Smith
I was born in 1948 a child of what George Orwell described as 'the lower upper middle class' which at that time found itself engaged in the dissolution of the British Empire. My early life therefore was military and nomadic. My earliest memories are of nearly drowning in a fish pond in Port Said and of standing on the lawn of a bungalow in Malaya while a bush fire ran through the long grass around the fence leaving the bungalow miraculously unharmed.

My schooling ranged through Preparatory and Direct Grant to Grammar and Comprehensive. I sold corsets on a market stall before reading Politics at Leeds University. After taking my degree I worked for the Simon Community romantically seeking lice and violence. I also worked in a wine cellar, as a lorry driver's mate and spent a year in accountancy. At present I am a teacher in London finding that my roots, like the British Empire, have vanished. My prep school is now a multi-storey car park.

Georgina Hammick
Georgina Hammick was born in Hampshire in 1939, and was educated at boarding schools in England and Kenya. Afterwards she did courses at the Academie Julian, Paris, and Salisbury Art School, and subsequently taught in various schools. She has written poetry intermittently since childhood, but only recently begun to work seriously. Married to Charles Hammick, bookseller, she has three children and lives in Long Sutton, Hampshire.

I. P. Taylor
Born 1946, Shipley, West Yorkshire. Educated at North Yorkshire grammar school and subsequently in a variety of

jobs, including night porter, car park attendant, Youth Hostel warden, gardener, farmworker, millhand, clerk and spent a most stimulating year as an unsuccessful smallholder in an isolated Yorkshire cottage: rearing goats, hens and apple trees. During the last eight years has lived in London, the Lake District, York, Wales and for the last two years in North Yorkshire. At present settled on the Yorkshire Wolds. Has been writing seriously since 1972. Poems published regularly in magazines. Was writing full time for a year upon returning to Yorkshire from Wales in 1974. Received a grant from the Yorkshire Arts Association in the same year. Won first prize in the 1975 Stroud Festival International Poetry Competition. Gives poetry readings. Is married with one son.